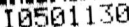

BUILDING BLOCKCHAIN DEVELOPMENT WITH ETHEREUM AND SOLIDITY

A STEP BY STEP HANDBOOK FOR CREATING DECENTRALIZED APPS AND SMART CONTRACTS ON ETHEREUM

IAN EBERT

COPYRIGHT

© [2024] by Ian Ebert All rights reserved.
No part of this publication may be reproduced, distributed, or transmitted in any form or by any means, including photocopying, recording, or other electronic or mechanical methods, without the prior written permission of the publisher, except in the case of brief quotations embodied in critical reviews and certain other noncommercial uses permitted by copyright law.

Disclaimer

The content presented in this book is for educational and informational purposes only. Every effort has been made to ensure the accuracy of the information at the time of publication; however, the author(s) and publisher make no representations or warranties about the completeness, accuracy, or current applicability of the material provided.

This book may include references to software, hardware, systems, or processes that are subject to change over time. Readers are encouraged to verify the information and ensure compatibility with their specific setups or environments before implementing any of the recommendations, instructions, or code snippets presented. Individual results may vary based on varying hardware, software versions, and user expertise.

The author(s) and publisher assume no liability for any errors, omissions, or outcomes that may arise from the application or use of the information in this book. The implementation of any techniques, processes, or configurations described herein is solely at the reader's own risk. It is recommended that users back up their data and systems and take necessary precautions before making any changes.

For complex technical challenges or if uncertainty arises, consulting with a qualified professional or technical expert is advisable.

Contents

Disclaimer..3

    Chapter 1: Introduction to Blockchain
Technology..10

        Overview of Blockchain Concepts.............. 10

        History and Evolution of Blockchain.......... 11

        Benefits and Challenges of Blockchain
Technology..12

    Chapter 2: Understanding Ethereum................. 14

        What is Ethereum?..14

        Key Features of the Ethereum Platform...... 14

        Ethereum vs. Bitcoin: A Comparative
Analysis.. 16

    Chapter 4: Getting Started with Solidity........... 18

        Introduction to Solidity Programming
Language..18

        Setting Up the Development Environment.. 18

        Basic Syntax and Data Types in Solidity.....20

    Chapter 5: Building Your First Smart Contract. 23

        Step-by-Step Guide to Creating a Simple
Smart Contract.. 23

            Step 1: Setting Up the Project................23

            Step 2: Writing the Smart Contract........24

            Step 3: Compiling the Smart Contract...25

            Step 4: Deploying the Smart Contract... 25

            Step 5: Interacting with the Smart
Contract...27

    Chapter 6: Advanced Solidity Concepts........... 29

        Inheritance and Interfaces in Solidity.......... 29

Inheritance.. 29
  Interfaces..31
  Libraries and Their Usage........................... 32
  Modifiers and Error Handling..................... 34
  Error Handling.. 35
Chapter 7: Testing Smart Contracts................... 37
  Importance of Testing in Blockchain Development...37
  Tools and Frameworks for Testing Solidity Contracts... 37
  Writing and Executing Unit Tests................38
    Step 1: Setting Up Test Files.................38
    Step 2: Writing Test Cases.................... 38
    Step 3: Running the Tests..................... 40
  Best Practices for Testing Smart Contracts..41
Chapter 8: Introduction to Decentralized Applications (dApps)..43
  What Are dApps?.. 43
  Architecture of dApps.................................43
  Differences Between dApps and Traditional Applications.. 44
  Use Cases for dApps...................................45
  Challenges Facing dApps............................ 45
Chapter 9: Interacting with Smart Contracts..... 48
  Overview of Contract Interaction................ 48
  Methods of Interacting with Smart Contracts.. 48

Setting Up Web3.js.................................... 49
Interacting with a Smart Contract Using Web3.js... 49
Using Metamask for Interaction................. 51
Best Practices for Contract Interaction........ 53

Chapter 10: Security Best Practices for Smart Contracts..55
Importance of Security in Smart Contracts. 55
Common Vulnerabilities............................. 55
Security Best Practices............................... 57
Tools for Security Analysis........................ 59

Chapter 11: Deploying Smart Contracts to the Ethereum Network..61
Overview of Deployment........................... 61
Preparing for Deployment.......................... 61
Deployment Steps....................................... 62
    Step 1: Write Migration Scripts............. 62
    Step 2: Compile Contracts..................... 63
    Step 3: Deploy to a Test Network.......... 63
    Step 4: Deploy to Mainnet..................... 64
Interacting with Deployed Contracts.......... 65
Best Practices for Deployment................... 65

Chapter 12: Managing Upgrades and Maintenance of Smart Contracts...................... 67
The Need for Upgradability....................... 67
Common Upgrade Patterns........................ 67
Considerations for Upgrading.................... 69

Governance and Control..............................70
Monitoring and Maintenance.......................70
Chapter 13: Integrating Oracles in Smart Contracts..72
Understanding Oracles.................................72
Types of Oracles.. 72
Popular Oracle Solutions............................. 73
Integrating Oracles into Smart Contracts.... 74
- Step 1: Install the Chainlink Library..... 74
- Step 2: Import the Oracle Interface....... 74
- Step 3: Create the Contract.................... 75
- Step 4: Deploy the Contract...................76
Use Cases for Oracles..................................76
Security Considerations..............................76
Chapter 14: Building User Interfaces for dApps...78
Introduction to dApp User Interfaces.......... 78
Popular Frameworks for dApp Development..78
Setting Up the Development Environment..79
Building the User Interface..........................80
User Experience Best Practices................... 82
Testing and Deployment.............................. 83
Chapter 15: Testing Smart Contracts.................85
Importance of Testing................................. 85
Testing Methodologies................................85
Tools for Testing Smart Contracts............... 86

Writing Tests in Truffle.................................86
Best Practices for Testing........................... 88
Security Testing.. 89
Chapter 16: Best Practices for Smart Contract Development..91
Importance of Best Practices....................... 91
Code Clarity and Documentation................ 91
Security Considerations.............................. 92
Testing and Auditing...................................93
Upgradeability and Maintenance................. 93
Efficient Gas Management.......................... 93
Decentralization and Transparency..............94
Compliance and Regulations....................... 95
Recap of Key Concepts Covered.......................95
Resources for Further Learning and Exploration.. 96
Encouragement to Contribute to the Blockchain Community.. 98

Chapter 1: Introduction to Blockchain Technology

Overview of Blockchain Concepts

Blockchain technology is a decentralized, distributed ledger system that enables secure and transparent record-keeping. At its core, a blockchain consists of a chain of blocks, each containing a list of transactions. These blocks are linked together in chronological order, forming an immutable chain. This design ensures that once data is recorded on the blockchain, it cannot be altered or deleted, enhancing trust among participants.

Key components of blockchain technology include:

Decentralization: Unlike traditional databases managed by a central authority, blockchains distribute data across a network of computers (nodes). This decentralization reduces the risk of single points of failure and enhances security.
Consensus Mechanisms: To validate transactions and add them to the blockchain, nodes must reach consensus. Common consensus algorithms include Proof of Work (PoW) and Proof of Stake (PoS), each with its own strengths and weaknesses.

Cryptography: Blockchain employs cryptographic techniques to secure data. Hash functions ensure the integrity of blocks, while public and private keys facilitate secure transactions between parties.

History and Evolution of Blockchain

The concept of blockchain was first introduced in 2008 by an anonymous person (or group) using the pseudonym Satoshi Nakamoto in the Bitcoin whitepaper. Bitcoin was designed as a peer-to-peer electronic cash system that would enable secure, digital transactions without the need for intermediaries like banks.

Since the launch of Bitcoin in 2009, the blockchain space has evolved significantly:

2015: Ethereum was introduced, allowing developers to create decentralized applications (dApps) and smart contracts. This expanded the potential use cases of blockchain beyond currency.
2017: The rise of Initial Coin Offerings (ICOs) fueled the growth of numerous blockchain projects, leading to increased interest in cryptocurrencies and decentralized finance (DeFi).
2020 and Beyond: The emergence of non-fungible tokens (NFTs), layer 2 scaling solutions, and decentralized autonomous organizations (DAOs) marked a new era in blockchain innovation.

Benefits and Challenges of Blockchain Technology

Benefits:

Transparency: Transactions on a blockchain are visible to all participants, fostering trust and accountability.
Security: The decentralized nature and cryptographic protections make blockchains resistant to tampering and fraud.
Efficiency: Blockchain can streamline processes by eliminating intermediaries, reducing costs and time.

Challenges:

Scalability: As more users join the network, maintaining performance and speed can become difficult.
Energy Consumption: Some consensus mechanisms, particularly PoW, require significant energy resources.
Regulatory Uncertainty: Governments worldwide are still defining how to regulate blockchain technology and cryptocurrencies, which can create uncertainty for developers and businesses.

In this chapter, we laid the foundation for understanding blockchain technology. By grasping its core concepts, history, and potential benefits and challenges, readers will be well-equipped to explore Ethereum and Solidity in subsequent chapters. Blockchain represents a transformative shift in how we think about data, trust, and collaboration, setting the stage for innovations that could reshape industries and societies.

Chapter 2: Understanding Ethereum

What is Ethereum?

Ethereum is an open-source, blockchain-based platform that enables developers to build and deploy decentralized applications (dApps) and smart contracts. Launched in 2015 by Vitalik Buterin and a team of developers, Ethereum expands the capabilities of blockchain beyond cryptocurrency, allowing for programmable and self-executing agreements. At its core, Ethereum functions as a global computer, providing the infrastructure for applications that can operate without intermediaries.

Key Features of the Ethereum Platform

Smart Contracts: Ethereum's most groundbreaking feature, smart contracts are self-executing contracts with the terms directly written into code. They automatically enforce and execute agreements when predefined conditions are met, eliminating the need for a trusted intermediary.

Decentralized Applications (dApps): Developers can create dApps on the Ethereum platform, which are applications that run on a decentralized network. These applications can serve various purposes, from finance to gaming, and leverage the security and transparency of the blockchain.

Ethereum Virtual Machine (EVM): The EVM is a runtime environment that allows smart contracts to be executed on the Ethereum network. It ensures that code is executed consistently across all nodes, creating a reliable environment for dApps.

Token Standards: Ethereum introduced various token standards, the most notable being ERC-20 and ERC-721. ERC-20 tokens are fungible, while ERC-721 tokens are unique and represent non-fungible assets (NFTs). These standards enable the creation of a vast ecosystem of tokens, enhancing the versatility of the platform.

Decentralized Finance (DeFi): Ethereum is the backbone of the DeFi movement, enabling financial services such as lending, borrowing, and trading without traditional financial intermediaries. DeFi protocols leverage smart contracts to provide these services, promoting financial inclusivity.

Ethereum vs. Bitcoin: A Comparative Analysis

While both Ethereum and Bitcoin are built on blockchain technology, they serve different purposes:

Purpose:

Bitcoin: Primarily designed as a digital currency and store of value, Bitcoin aims to enable peer-to-peer transactions without intermediaries.

Ethereum: A platform for building decentralized applications and executing smart contracts, Ethereum goes beyond currency, facilitating various programmable transactions.

Transaction Speed:

Bitcoin: Typically processes transactions every 10 minutes.

Ethereum: Offers faster transaction times, averaging around 15 seconds, making it more suitable for real-time applications.

Supply:

Bitcoin: Has a capped supply of 21 million coins, creating scarcity.

Ethereum: Does not have a fixed supply, allowing for flexibility in its monetary policy.

Development Community:

Bitcoin: Focuses primarily on security and stability.

Ethereum: Encourages innovation and experimentation, fostering a vibrant developer community that continuously builds new applications and protocols.

In this chapter, we explored the essential aspects of Ethereum, highlighting its role as a powerful platform for decentralized applications and smart contracts.

Understanding Ethereum's unique features, along with its differences from Bitcoin, lays the groundwork for diving deeper into Solidity and the development of innovative applications in the following chapters. As Ethereum continues to evolve, it remains at the forefront of the blockchain revolution, driving significant advancements across various industries.

Chapter 4: Getting Started with Solidity

Introduction to Solidity Programming Language

Solidity is a high-level programming language specifically designed for writing smart contracts on the Ethereum blockchain. Developed by Christian Reitwiessner and a team of contributors, Solidity resembles JavaScript in syntax, making it relatively accessible for developers familiar with web technologies. It allows developers to create complex, self-executing agreements that run on the Ethereum Virtual Machine (EVM).

Setting Up the Development Environment

To start developing with Solidity, you need to set up your development environment. Here are the key components:

Node.js: Ensure you have Node.js installed on your machine. This will allow you to run JavaScript tools and packages essential for blockchain development.

Truffle Suite: Truffle is a popular development framework for Ethereum that simplifies the process of building and deploying smart contracts. To install Truffle, run:

bash
Copy code
```
npm install -g truffle
```

Ganache: Ganache is a personal Ethereum blockchain that you can use to deploy contracts, develop applications, and run tests. It simulates the blockchain locally. You can download Ganache from the Truffle Suite website or install it via npm:
bash
Copy code
```
npm install -g ganache-cli
```

Metamask: Metamask is a browser extension that acts as a cryptocurrency wallet and allows you to interact with the Ethereum blockchain. It's essential for testing dApps and managing your Ethereum accounts.

IDE (Integrated Development Environment): While you can use any text editor, online IDEs like Remix provide a convenient environment to write, test, and deploy Solidity contracts without any local setup.

Basic Syntax and Data Types in Solidity

Understanding Solidity's syntax and data types is crucial for writing effective smart contracts. Here's an overview of the fundamental components:

Contract Definition: A smart contract is defined using the `contract` keyword. Each contract can contain state variables, functions, and events.
solidity
Copy code
```
pragma solidity ^0.8.0;

contract SimpleStorage {
uint public storedData;
}
```

Data Types:
Value Types: Includes integers (`uint`, `int`), booleans (`bool`), and addresses (`address`).
Reference Types: Includes strings (`string`), arrays (`uint[]`), and mappings (`mapping(address => uint)`).
Structs: User-defined types that allow you to group related data.

```solidity
Copy code
struct Person {
string name;
uint age;
}
```

State Variables and Functions: State variables are stored on the blockchain, while functions can modify these variables or perform other operations.

```solidity
Copy code
function set(uint x) public {
storedData = x;
}

function get() public view returns (uint) {
return storedData;
}
```

Visibility Modifiers: These define the accessibility of functions and variables:

`public`: Accessible from outside the contract.

`private`: Accessible only within the contract.

`internal`: Accessible within the contract and derived contracts.

`external`: Accessible only from outside the contract.

In this chapter, we introduced Solidity, the programming language that enables developers to create smart contracts on the Ethereum blockchain. By setting up a development environment and understanding the basic syntax and data types, readers are prepared to dive deeper into writing and deploying their first smart contracts. The skills gained here will serve as a foundation for the subsequent chapters, where we will build more complex contracts and explore the broader ecosystem of Ethereum development.

Chapter 5: Building Your First Smart Contract

Step-by-Step Guide to Creating a Simple Smart Contract

In this chapter, we will walk through the process of creating, deploying, and interacting with a simple smart contract on the Ethereum blockchain. Our example will be a basic storage contract that allows users to store and retrieve a single integer value.

Step 1: Setting Up the Project

Create a New Directory: Start by creating a new directory for your project and navigate into it.
bash
Copy code
```
mkdir SimpleStorage
cd SimpleStorage
```

Initialize a Truffle Project: Run the following command to create a new Truffle project:
bash
Copy code
```
truffle init
```

Install Dependencies: If you need any additional libraries or tools, you can install them using npm. For now, Truffle will handle most of your needs.

Step 2: Writing the Smart Contract

Create a New Solidity File: Inside the `contracts` directory, create a file named `SimpleStorage.sol`.

Define the Contract: Open `SimpleStorage.sol` and add the following code:
solidity
Copy code

```solidity
// SPDX-License-Identifier: MIT
pragma solidity ^0.8.0;

contract SimpleStorage {
uint private storedData;

// Function to set the value
function set(uint x) public {
storedData = x;
}

// Function to retrieve the value
function get() public view returns (uint) {
return storedData;
}
}
```

Step 3: Compiling the Smart Contract

Compile the Contract: Run the following command to compile your contract:
bash
Copy code
```
truffle compile
```

This command generates the necessary artifacts, including the Application Binary Interface (ABI) and bytecode.

Step 4: Deploying the Smart Contract

Create a Migration Script: In the `migrations` directory, create a new file named `2_deploy_contracts.js` and add the following code:
javascript
Copy code
```javascript
const SimpleStorage = artifacts.require("SimpleStorage");

module.exports = function (deployer) {
  deployer.deploy(SimpleStorage);
};
```

Run Ganache: Start a local Ethereum blockchain using Ganache. Open another terminal and run:

bash
Copy code
```
ganache-cli
```

This will create a local blockchain instance.

Deploy the Contract: In your original terminal, run:
bash
Copy code
```
truffle migrate
```

This command deploys your contract to the Ganache blockchain. You should see output indicating that the contract has been deployed successfully.

Step 5: Interacting with the Smart Contract

Open Truffle Console: Start the Truffle console by running:
bash
Copy code
```
truffle console
```

Interact with the Contract: In the console, you can interact with your deployed contract. First, get an instance of the contract:
javascript
Copy code

```
let instance = await SimpleStorage.deployed();
```

Set a Value: Use the `set` function to store a value:
javascript
Copy code
```
await instance.set(42);
```

Retrieve the Value: Now, use the `get` function to retrieve the stored value:
javascript
Copy code
```
let value = await instance.get();
console.log(value.toString());   // Should output '42'
```

Congratulations! You have successfully created, deployed, and interacted with your first smart contract on the Ethereum blockchain. This basic storage contract demonstrates the core concepts of writing and using smart contracts, including defining functions, setting and retrieving data, and deploying to the blockchain.

In the following chapters, we will explore more advanced Solidity concepts and dive deeper into building more complex decentralized applications (dApps). By mastering these fundamentals, you will be well-equipped to leverage the full potential of Ethereum and its ecosystem.

Chapter 6: Advanced Solidity Concepts

Inheritance and Interfaces in Solidity

One of the powerful features of Solidity is its support for inheritance, allowing developers to create more complex and modular smart contracts. Inheritance lets you define a base contract and extend it with additional functionality in derived contracts. This promotes code reuse and reduces redundancy.

Inheritance
Base Contract: Define a base contract with common functionalities.
solidity

Copy code
```
contract Animal {
string public species;

constructor(string memory _species) {
species = _species;
}

function getSpecies() public view returns (string memory) {
return species;
}
}
```

Derived Contract: Create a derived contract that inherits from the base contract.
solidity
Copy code
```
contract Dog is Animal {
string public name;

constructor(string memory _name) Animal("Dog") {
name = _name;
```

```
}

function getName() public view returns (string memory) {
return name;
}
}
```

In this example, the `Dog` contract inherits properties and functions from the `Animal` contract, allowing it to utilize and extend its functionality.

Interfaces

Interfaces define a contract's function signatures without providing implementations. They allow contracts to interact with one another while enforcing a consistent structure.

Define an Interface:
solidity
Copy code
```
interface IAnimal {
function getSpecies() external view returns (string memory);
}
```

Implement the Interface:
solidity
Copy code
```
contract Cat is IAnimal {
string public species;

constructor() {
species = "Cat";
}

function getSpecies() public view override returns (string memory) {
return species;
}
}
```

The `Cat` contract implements the `IAnimal` interface, ensuring it provides the required function.

Libraries and Their Usage

Libraries in Solidity are collections of reusable code that can be called from contracts. They help in organizing code and reducing deployment costs since they are deployed only once and can be used by multiple contracts.

Creating a Library:
solidity
Copy code
```
library Math {
function add(uint a, uint b) internal pure returns (uint) {
return a + b;
}
}
```

Using a Library:
solidity
Copy code
```
contract Calculator {
using Math for uint;

function calculateSum(uint a, uint b) public pure returns (uint) {
return a.add(b);
}
}
```

In this example, the `Calculator` contract uses the `Math` library to perform addition, showcasing how libraries enhance code modularity.

Modifiers and Error Handling

Modifiers are special functions that can alter the behavior of other functions. They are often used for access control or validation.

Creating a Modifier:
solidity
Copy code
```
modifier onlyOwner() {
require(msg.sender == owner, "Not the owner");
_;
}
```

Applying a Modifier:
solidity
Copy code
```
contract Owned {
address public owner;
```

```
constructor() {
owner = msg.sender;
}

function restrictedFunction() public
onlyOwner {
// Only the owner can call this
function
}
}
```

The `onlyOwner` modifier checks that the caller is the owner before executing the function.

Error Handling

Solidity provides mechanisms for error handling using `require`, `assert`, and `revert`:

require: Used to validate inputs or conditions. If the condition is false, it reverts the transaction.
assert: Used to check for internal errors. If it fails, it indicates a bug in the contract.
revert: Used to manually revert transactions and can provide error messages.

In this chapter, we explored advanced Solidity concepts, including inheritance, interfaces, libraries, modifiers, and error handling. Mastering these concepts allows developers to create more efficient, modular, and secure smart contracts. As we move forward, these principles will be essential for building complex dApps and utilizing the full potential of Ethereum's capabilities.

Chapter 7: Testing Smart Contracts

Importance of Testing in Blockchain Development

Testing smart contracts is crucial due to the immutable nature of blockchain technology. Once deployed, contracts cannot be altered, making thorough testing essential to ensure security, correctness, and functionality. Bugs or vulnerabilities in smart contracts can lead to significant financial losses, making it imperative to adopt a rigorous testing process.

Tools and Frameworks for Testing Solidity Contracts

Truffle Framework: Truffle provides a robust testing framework that integrates seamlessly with your development environment. It supports both JavaScript and Solidity tests.

Ganache: A personal Ethereum blockchain for testing, Ganache allows developers to deploy contracts and run tests in a controlled environment.

Chai: An assertion library often used with Truffle tests to enhance readability and expressiveness in test cases.

Hardhat: An alternative to Truffle that offers a flexible environment for Ethereum development, including built-in testing support.

Writing and Executing Unit Tests

To ensure your smart contracts function correctly, you'll want to write unit tests. Here's a step-by-step guide:

Step 1: Setting Up Test Files

Create a Test Directory: In your Truffle project, navigate to the `test` directory. Create a new file named `SimpleStorage.test.js`.

Import the Contract: At the top of your test file, import your smart contract:
javascript
Copy code
```
const SimpleStorage = artifacts.require("SimpleStorage");
```

Step 2: Writing Test Cases

Describe the Test Suite: Use the Mocha framework (integrated with Truffle) to describe your test cases:
javascript
Copy code
```
contract("SimpleStorage", accounts => {
let simpleStorage;
```

```javascript
before(async () => {
  simpleStorage = await SimpleStorage.deployed();
});

it("should store a value", async () => {
  await simpleStorage.set(42);
  const value = await simpleStorage.get();
  assert.equal(value.toString(), '42', "The stored value should be 42");
});

it("should return 0 initially", async () => {
  const value = await simpleStorage.get();
  assert.equal(value.toString(), '0', "The initial stored value should be 0");
});
});
```

In this example, we created two test cases: one to check that the contract correctly stores a value and another to confirm the initial state.

Step 3: Running the Tests

Execute Tests: Run the following command in your terminal to execute your tests:
bash
Copy code
```
truffle test
```

Truffle will compile the contracts, deploy them to Ganache, and run your tests. You should see the output indicating whether each test passed or failed.

Best Practices for Testing Smart Contracts

Test All Functions: Ensure that every function, including edge cases, is tested. This includes failure paths and conditions.

Use Descriptive Assertions: Clearly describe what each test checks. This helps in understanding failures and maintaining tests over time.

Isolate Tests: Each test should be independent of others to avoid interference. Use the `beforeEach` hook if necessary to reset state.

Automate Testing: Integrate your testing suite into your development workflow. Use Continuous Integration (CI) tools to automate testing during code changes.

Gas Usage Tests: Monitor the gas consumption of your functions to ensure they remain efficient and cost-effective.

In this chapter, we emphasized the importance of testing in smart contract development and provided a comprehensive guide on writing and executing tests using Truffle. By adopting rigorous testing practices, developers can significantly reduce the risk of vulnerabilities and ensure that their contracts behave as intended. As we progress, the ability to effectively test smart contracts will be crucial for building robust and reliable decentralized applications.

Chapter 8: Introduction to Decentralized Applications (dApps)

What Are dApps?

Decentralized applications, or dApps, are applications that run on a decentralized network, utilizing blockchain technology to operate without a central authority. Unlike traditional applications that rely on centralized servers, dApps leverage smart contracts on platforms like Ethereum to facilitate peer-to-peer interactions, enhance security, and ensure transparency. This architecture allows for a wide range of applications, from finance and gaming to social networking and supply chain management.

Architecture of dApps

The architecture of a dApp typically consists of three layers:

Frontend: The user interface where users interact with the dApp. This can be built using standard web technologies (HTML, CSS, JavaScript) and frameworks like React or Vue.js.

Smart Contracts: The backend logic that governs the application's behavior, executed on the blockchain. Smart contracts handle the business logic, data storage, and interactions between users.

Blockchain: The underlying distributed ledger that records all transactions and ensures data integrity. Ethereum serves as the most popular platform for deploying smart contracts.

Differences Between dApps and Traditional Applications

Decentralization: dApps operate on a decentralized network, reducing the risks associated with single points of failure. Traditional applications rely on central servers and databases.

Transparency: All transactions on the blockchain are publicly visible, providing transparency and accountability. Traditional applications may operate behind closed doors, with limited user visibility into data handling.

Security: dApps benefit from blockchain's cryptographic security, making them resistant to tampering and fraud. Traditional applications can be vulnerable to hacks and data breaches.

Ownership: Users often have more control and ownership over their data in dApps, as they are typically designed to allow users to manage their information directly.

Use Cases for dApps

Decentralized Finance (DeFi): Platforms that provide financial services like lending, borrowing, and trading without intermediaries (e.g., Aave, Uniswap).
Gaming: Blockchain-based games where players can own and trade in-game assets as NFTs (e.g., Axie Infinity, Cryptokitties).
Social Media: Decentralized social networks that prioritize user privacy and data ownership (e.g., Mastodon, Diaspora).
Supply Chain Management: dApps that enhance traceability and transparency in supply chains by recording every step on the blockchain (e.g., VeChain).
Voting Systems: Secure and transparent voting mechanisms built on blockchain to ensure integrity and trust in electoral processes.

Challenges Facing dApps

User Experience: The complexity of blockchain technology can lead to a steep learning curve for users. Improving the usability and accessibility of dApps is essential for widespread adoption.
Scalability: Many blockchain networks face challenges with scalability, impacting transaction speed and cost during peak usage times.

Regulatory Uncertainty: The legal landscape for dApps and cryptocurrencies is still evolving, leading to uncertainties for developers and users alike.

Interoperability: The ability for dApps to communicate and operate across different blockchains is still a developing area, posing challenges for developers.

In this chapter, we introduced decentralized applications (dApps) and discussed their architecture, differences from traditional applications, use cases, and associated challenges. Understanding the fundamentals of dApps is crucial as we move forward in exploring the development of these innovative applications using Ethereum and Solidity. As blockchain technology matures, dApps hold the potential to revolutionize various industries by offering more secure, transparent, and user-centric solutions.

Chapter 9: Interacting with Smart Contracts

Overview of Contract Interaction

Interacting with smart contracts involves sending transactions and calling functions defined in the contract. This interaction is fundamental to building decentralized applications (dApps), allowing users to execute actions, read data, and participate in the application's logic on the Ethereum blockchain.

Methods of Interacting with Smart Contracts

Direct Transactions: Users can directly call functions on smart contracts by sending transactions. This method is common for state-changing functions.

Read-Only Calls: For functions that do not change the state (view or pure functions), users can make calls that do not require sending a transaction. These calls are less costly and can be executed instantly.

Web3.js Library: Web3.js is a popular JavaScript library that enables interaction with the Ethereum blockchain and smart contracts. It allows developers to build user interfaces for dApps that can read from and write to smart contracts.

Setting Up Web3.js

Installation: First, install Web3.js via npm:
bash
Copy code
```
npm install web3
```

Connecting to the Ethereum Network: Use Web3.js to connect to a local or remote Ethereum node. For local development, you can connect to Ganache:
javascript
Copy code
```
const Web3 = require('web3');
const web3 = new Web3('http://localhost:7545'); // Ganache default URL
```

Interacting with a Smart Contract Using Web3.js

Getting the Contract ABI and Address: After deploying your contract, retrieve its ABI (Application Binary Interface) and contract address. The ABI defines the contract's functions and structure.

Creating a Contract Instance:
javascript
Copy code

```
const contractAddress = 'YOUR_CONTRACT_ADDRESS';
const contractABI = [ /* Your ABI here */ ];

const contract = new web3.eth.Contract(contractABI, contractAddress);
```

Calling Functions:

Read Data: Use the `call` method for read-only functions.

javascript
Copy code
```
contract.methods.get().call()
.then(result => {
console.log(result); // Outputs the stored value
});
```

Sending Transactions: Use the `send` method for state-changing functions.

javascript
Copy code
```
const account = 'YOUR_ACCOUNT_ADDRESS';

contract.methods.set(42).send({ from: account })
.then(receipt => {
console.log(receipt); // Transaction receipt
})
.catch(error => {
console.error(error);
});
```

Using Metamask for Interaction

Metamask is a browser extension that acts as a wallet and allows users to interact with dApps securely:

Install Metamask: Download and install the Metamask extension in your browser.

Connect Metamask to Your dApp: Use the following code to prompt users to connect their Metamask wallet:
javascript

Copy code
```
async function connectWallet() {
if (window.ethereum) {
await window.ethereum.request({ method: 'eth_requestAccounts' });
const accounts = await web3.eth.getAccounts();
console.log('Connected account:', accounts[0]);
} else {
console.error('Metamask is not installed!');
}
}
```

Interacting with the Contract: Once connected, you can use the same Web3.js methods to interact with your smart contract.

Best Practices for Contract Interaction

Handle Errors Gracefully: Always include error handling for contract interactions to manage issues that may arise from failed transactions or network problems.

Gas Management: Be mindful of gas limits and prices when sending transactions. Consider implementing mechanisms to estimate gas requirements.
User Feedback: Provide users with feedback on transaction statuses, including pending, success, and failure notifications.
Security: Ensure that the smart contracts are thoroughly tested and audited to prevent vulnerabilities.

In this chapter, we explored how to interact with smart contracts using Web3.js and Metamask, detailing the steps to set up connections, call functions, and manage user accounts. Understanding these interaction methods is essential for building responsive and engaging dApps. As we continue our exploration of Ethereum and Solidity, these skills will serve as the backbone for creating rich, user-friendly applications that harness the power of blockchain technology.

Chapter 10: Security Best Practices for Smart Contracts

Importance of Security in Smart Contracts

Smart contracts are immutable once deployed, meaning any vulnerabilities or bugs can lead to irreversible consequences, including financial losses. Ensuring the security of smart contracts is critical, especially as they often manage significant assets and sensitive data. This chapter outlines best practices for developing secure smart contracts and mitigating common vulnerabilities.

Common Vulnerabilities

Reentrancy Attacks: This occurs when a function makes an external call to another contract before it finishes executing, allowing the called contract to re-enter and manipulate the state unexpectedly.
Mitigation: Use the Checks-Effects-Interactions pattern. Always update state variables before calling external contracts.

solidity
Copy code

```
function withdraw(uint amount) public
{
require(balances[msg.sender]        >=
amount);
balances[msg.sender] -= amount;
payable(msg.sender).transfer(amount);
// External call
}
```

Integer Overflow and Underflow: Arithmetic operations that exceed the maximum or minimum limits can cause unexpected behavior.
Mitigation: Use the SafeMath library to handle arithmetic operations safely.

solidity
Copy code
```
using SafeMath for uint;

function add(uint a, uint b) public
pure returns (uint) {
return a.add(b); // Safe addition
}
```

Access Control Issues: Improperly managed permissions can allow unauthorized users to execute sensitive functions.

Mitigation: Use modifiers to enforce access control. Implement role-based access control where necessary.

solidity
Copy code
```
modifier onlyOwner() {
require(msg.sender == owner, "Not the owner");
_;
}
```

Gas Limit and Loops: Contracts that perform extensive computations or use unbounded loops can exceed gas limits, causing transactions to fail.

Mitigation: Avoid complex computations in contracts and use external services or off-chain solutions for heavy calculations.

Security Best Practices

Code Audits: Regularly conduct internal and external audits of your smart contracts. This helps identify vulnerabilities and improves code quality.

Testing: Implement extensive unit and integration tests. Use frameworks like Truffle or Hardhat to simulate different scenarios and edge cases.

Use of Established Libraries: Leverage well-audited libraries (like OpenZeppelin) for common functionalities, such as token standards and access control.

Fail-Safe Mechanisms: Implement circuit breakers or emergency stop functions that can pause contract operations in case of a detected vulnerability.

solidity
Copy code
```
bool public stopped;

modifier stopInEmergency {
require(!stopped);
_;
}

function toggleContractActive() public onlyOwner {
stopped = !stopped;
}
```

Minimize State Variables: Keep state variables to a minimum. Reducing complexity can help limit potential attack vectors.

Events for Transparency: Use events to log significant state changes. This provides transparency and aids in auditing contract behavior.

solidity
Copy code
```
event Withdraw(address indexed user, uint amount);
```

Tools for Security Analysis

MythX: A security analysis tool that identifies vulnerabilities in smart contracts using automated analysis.
Slither: A static analysis tool for Solidity that detects potential vulnerabilities and provides insights into code quality.
Remix IDE: Offers built-in static analysis tools that highlight potential security issues during development.

In this chapter, we emphasized the importance of security in smart contract development and outlined common vulnerabilities and best practices for mitigating risks. By adhering to these principles and leveraging available tools, developers can significantly enhance the security of their smart contracts. As we continue to build decentralized applications, prioritizing security will ensure trust and integrity in the blockchain ecosystem.

Chapter 11: Deploying Smart Contracts to the Ethereum Network

Overview of Deployment

Deploying smart contracts to the Ethereum network is the process of publishing your contract to the blockchain, making it accessible for interaction by users and other contracts. This chapter will guide you through the deployment process, from preparation to mainnet deployment.

Preparing for Deployment

Choose the Right Network: Decide whether to deploy on a test network (like Ropsten, Rinkeby, or Kovan) for testing or directly on the Ethereum mainnet for production. Test networks simulate the mainnet environment and are ideal for trial runs.

Configure Your Environment: Ensure you have your development environment set up, including Truffle, Ganache, or Hardhat. Install Web3.js or ethers.js for interacting with Ethereum.

Set Up a Wallet: Use a wallet like MetaMask or create a wallet programmatically to manage your Ethereum account and handle transactions.

Acquire Ether: For mainnet deployments, ensure your wallet has enough Ether to cover gas fees. You can obtain test Ether from faucets for test networks.

Deployment Steps

Step 1: Write Migration Scripts

Migration scripts automate the deployment process. In Truffle, create a new migration file in the `migrations` directory:

javascript
Copy code
```
const SimpleStorage = artifacts.require("SimpleStorage");

module.exports = function (deployer) {
  deployer.deploy(SimpleStorage);
};
```

Step 2: Compile Contracts

Compile your contracts to ensure there are no syntax errors:

```bash
truffle compile
```

Step 3: Deploy to a Test Network

Configure the Truffle Network: Update the `truffle-config.js` file to include your desired network settings.

```javascript
networks: {
  ropsten: {
    provider: () => new HDWalletProvider(mnemonic, `https://ropsten.infura.io/v3/YOUR_INFURA_PROJECT_ID`),
    network_id: 3,        // Ropsten's id
    gas: 5500000,         // Gas limit
  },
},
```

Deploy the Contract:

```bash
```

Copy code
```
truffle migrate --network ropsten
```

This command deploys your contracts to the Ropsten test network. Monitor the output for transaction hashes and confirmation of deployment.

Step 4: Deploy to Mainnet

After successful testing on the testnet:

Update Configuration: Adjust your `truffle-config.js` to include the mainnet settings.

javascript
Copy code
```
mainnet: {
provider: () => new HDWalletProvider(mnemonic,
`https://mainnet.infura.io/v3/YOUR_INFURA_PROJECT_ID`),
network_id: 1,      // Mainnet's id
gas: 5500000,       // Gas limit
},
```

Deploy to Mainnet:

```bash
Copy code
truffle migrate --network mainnet
```

This will publish your contract to the Ethereum mainnet.

Interacting with Deployed Contracts

Once deployed, you can interact with your contract using Web3.js or ethers.js. Retrieve the contract instance using its address and ABI, similar to how we did in Chapter 9.

Best Practices for Deployment

Thorough Testing: Ensure all functionality is rigorously tested on test networks before mainnet deployment.
Gas Estimation: Use tools to estimate gas costs for transactions to avoid running out of gas during deployment.
Monitor Transactions: Use blockchain explorers like Etherscan to track deployment transactions and contract interactions.
Security Checks: Conduct security audits and thorough code reviews before deploying to avoid vulnerabilities.
Keep Contracts Upgradable: Consider implementing proxy patterns or upgradable contracts to facilitate future changes without losing the contract state.

In this chapter, we outlined the deployment process for smart contracts on the Ethereum network, covering preparations, migration scripts, and best practices. Deploying to both test networks and the mainnet requires careful consideration and testing to ensure success. With a solid understanding of deployment, you can confidently launch your decentralized applications, contributing to the evolving blockchain ecosystem.

Chapter 12: Managing Upgrades and Maintenance of Smart Contracts

The Need for Upgradability

Smart contracts, once deployed, are immutable. This means that any bugs, vulnerabilities, or required feature enhancements cannot be altered directly. Upgradability becomes essential in maintaining the contract's relevance and security. This chapter discusses various strategies for managing upgrades and maintaining smart contracts effectively.

Common Upgrade Patterns

Proxy Pattern: The most popular method for upgradability. This involves deploying a proxy contract that delegates calls to a logic contract. The logic contract can be updated while preserving the proxy's state.
How It Works:
Proxy Contract: Holds the state and delegates calls to the implementation contract.
Logic Contract: Contains the contract's business logic.

Upgrades involve deploying a new logic contract and updating the proxy to point to it.
Example:

```solidity
contract Proxy {
    address implementation;

    function upgradeTo(address newImplementation) external {
        implementation = newImplementation;
    }

    fallback() external {
        (bool success, ) = implementation.delegatecall(msg.data);
        require(success);
    }
}
```

Eternal Storage Pattern: Separates state storage from business logic, allowing the logic contract to be upgraded without losing the stored data.
How It Works:

An Eternal Storage contract handles all state variables.
The main contract uses this storage to retrieve and set values.

Upgrading involves deploying a new version of the logic contract while the storage remains unchanged.

Clones and Minimal Proxies: This approach uses a factory contract to deploy clones of a base contract, reducing deployment costs. Each clone can have its state but shares the logic.

Benefits: Cost-effective and allows for creating multiple instances that can be upgraded individually.

Considerations for Upgrading

State Preservation: Ensure that the state remains intact during upgrades. Design contracts with upgradability in mind from the outset.

Security Audits: Every time a contract is upgraded, conduct a security audit. New implementations can introduce vulnerabilities.

Migration Scripts: Write migration scripts to facilitate the upgrade process and handle any necessary data migrations.

Transparency and Communication: Clearly communicate upgrade intentions to users. Maintain transparency about changes to preserve trust.

Testing Upgrades: Rigorously test upgrades in a staging environment before deploying them on the mainnet.

Governance and Control

Multisig Wallets: Use multisignature wallets to control upgrade processes, ensuring that multiple parties approve any changes, enhancing security.
Decentralized Governance: Consider implementing governance tokens that allow stakeholders to vote on contract upgrades, fostering community involvement.

Monitoring and Maintenance

Continuous Monitoring: After deployment, continuously monitor contract performance and security. Tools like Etherscan and Tenderly can help track transactions and detect anomalies.
Bug Bounty Programs: Launch bug bounty programs to incentivize white-hat hackers to discover vulnerabilities before malicious actors do.
Regular Updates: Stay informed about Ethereum protocol updates and community best practices. Regularly review and update contracts to align with new standards.

In this chapter, we discussed the importance of managing upgrades and maintenance for smart contracts. By employing strategies such as the proxy pattern, eternal storage, and clones, developers can ensure their contracts remain flexible and relevant. Prioritizing security, transparency, and community involvement will further enhance the trustworthiness of deployed contracts. As the blockchain landscape evolves, effective upgrade and maintenance practices will be crucial for the longevity and success of decentralized applications.

Chapter 13: Integrating Oracles in Smart Contracts

Understanding Oracles

Oracles are third-party services that provide smart contracts with external data from the real world. They act as bridges between the blockchain and external systems, enabling contracts to react to real-time information. This capability is vital for many decentralized applications (dApps) that require data inputs beyond what the blockchain natively provides, such as price feeds, weather data, and event results.

Types of Oracles

Centralized Oracles: Operated by a single entity that sources and provides data to smart contracts. While simpler to implement, they introduce a single point of failure and can compromise decentralization.
Decentralized Oracles: Aggregate data from multiple sources, reducing the risk of manipulation and improving reliability. These oracles utilize a consensus mechanism to ensure data accuracy.

Inbound Oracles: Provide data from external sources to the blockchain, such as market prices or sensor data.

Outbound Oracles: Allow smart contracts to trigger actions in the external world, such as sending notifications or executing transactions outside the blockchain.

Software Oracles: Fetch data from online sources, such as APIs, websites, or databases.

Hardware Oracles: Collect data from the physical world using sensors or IoT devices.

Popular Oracle Solutions

Chainlink: A decentralized oracle network that connects smart contracts with off-chain data securely and reliably. It uses multiple data sources and aggregators to ensure data integrity.

Band Protocol: A cross-chain data oracle platform that aggregates and connects real-world data and APIs to smart contracts. It focuses on scalability and decentralization.

API3: Allows decentralized APIs to directly connect with smart contracts without needing a third-party oracle. This enables greater trust and transparency.

Integrating Oracles into Smart Contracts

To integrate an oracle like Chainlink, follow these steps:

Step 1: Install the Chainlink Library

Use npm to install the Chainlink contracts library:

bash
Copy code
```
npm install @chainlink/contracts
```

Step 2: Import the Oracle Interface

In your smart contract, import the Chainlink Oracle interface:

solidity
Copy code
```
import "@chainlink/contracts/src/v0.8/interfaces/AggregatorV3Interface.sol";
```

Step 3: Create the Contract

Define your contract and the oracle interface:

solidity
Copy code
```
contract PriceConsumer {
AggregatorV3Interface       internal priceFeed;
```

```
constructor() {
priceFeed                        =
AggregatorV3Interface(0xYOUR_ORACLE_AD
DRESS);
}

function getLatestPrice() public view
returns (int) {
(
,
int price,
,
,
) = priceFeed.latestRoundData();
return price;
}
}
```

Replace 0xYOUR_ORACLE_ADDRESS with the actual address of the oracle you want to use.

Step 4: Deploy the Contract

Compile and deploy your contract to the Ethereum network, making sure to configure any necessary oracle addresses.

Use Cases for Oracles

DeFi Applications: Oracles provide real-time price feeds for cryptocurrencies and assets, enabling protocols to function correctly.
Insurance Contracts: Oracles can verify external conditions (e.g., weather data) to trigger insurance payouts.
Gaming: Real-world events can be used to determine outcomes in games or competitions, ensuring fair play.
Supply Chain: Oracles can track and confirm the status of goods in transit, enhancing transparency and trust.

Security Considerations

Data Integrity: Ensure that the oracle you choose has a good reputation and a proven track record for providing accurate and reliable data.
Decentralization: Prefer decentralized oracles to mitigate the risk of single points of failure.
Fallback Mechanisms: Implement fallback mechanisms in your contracts to handle scenarios where oracle data is unavailable or inconsistent.

Regular Audits: Regularly audit your oracle integration and contract logic to identify potential vulnerabilities or weaknesses.

In this chapter, we explored the role of oracles in smart contracts, discussing their types, popular solutions, and integration steps. Oracles enable smart contracts to interact with real-world data, expanding their functionality and applicability across various domains. Understanding how to effectively implement and secure oracle integrations is vital for developers looking to build robust and versatile decentralized applications. As the ecosystem evolves, oracles will continue to play a crucial role in bridging the gap between the blockchain and the real world.

Chapter 14: Building User Interfaces for dApps

Introduction to dApp User Interfaces

A well-designed user interface (UI) is crucial for the success of any decentralized application (dApp). The UI serves as the bridge between users and the underlying smart contracts, facilitating interactions in a seamless and intuitive manner. This chapter explores best practices for building user interfaces for dApps, focusing on frameworks, design principles, and integration with blockchain technology.

Popular Frameworks for dApp Development

React: A widely used JavaScript library for building user interfaces. Its component-based architecture allows for the creation of dynamic and interactive UIs.
Vue.js: Another progressive JavaScript framework that is easy to integrate into projects. Vue offers a flexible and approachable API for building responsive user interfaces.
Angular: A platform and framework for building single-page applications. Angular provides a robust structure for developing complex UIs with a focus on modularity.
Web3.js: A JavaScript library that allows developers to interact with the Ethereum blockchain. It is essential for connecting your UI to smart contracts.
Ethers.js: A lightweight alternative to Web3.js, offering similar functionality but with a more modern API design.

Setting Up the Development Environment
Create a React App: Use Create React App to bootstrap your project:
bash

Copy code
```
npx create-react-app my-dapp
cd my-dapp
```

Install Dependencies: Add necessary libraries like Web3.js or Ethers.js:
bash
Copy code
```
npm install ethers
```

Setting Up Metamask: Instruct users to install the MetaMask browser extension to manage their Ethereum accounts.

Building the User Interface

Designing Components: Break down your UI into reusable components. For example, create separate components for buttons, forms, and displays.
jsx
Copy code
```
function ConnectButton({ onClick }) {
    return <button onClick={onClick}>Connect Wallet</button>;
}
```

State Management: Use React's state management to track user inputs and contract data. Consider using Context API or libraries like Redux for larger applications.

Connecting to Smart Contracts:

Import the contract's ABI and address.

javascript
Copy code
```
import { ethers } from 'ethers';
import MyContract from './MyContract.json';

const contractAddress = 'YOUR_CONTRACT_ADDRESS';
const contractABI = MyContract.abi;
```

Initialize the connection in your component:

javascript
Copy code
```
async function connectContract() {
if (typeof window.ethereum !== 'undefined') {
```

```
const provider = new ethers.providers.Web3Provider(window.ethereum);
const signer = provider.getSigner();
const contract = new ethers.Contract(contractAddress, contractABI, signer);
// Interact with the contract
  }
}
```

Handling User Interactions: Implement functions to handle user inputs and trigger smart contract interactions, such as sending transactions or fetching data.

javascript
Copy code
```
async function setValue(newValue) {
  const tx = await contract.set(newValue);
  await tx.wait();
  // Update UI after transaction
}
```

User Experience Best Practices

Clear Navigation: Ensure users can easily navigate the dApp. Use a consistent layout and clear calls-to-action.

Loading Indicators: Provide visual feedback during transactions, such as spinners or status messages, to inform users that their action is being processed.

Error Handling: Implement robust error handling to display user-friendly messages when transactions fail or if the user's wallet is not connected.

Responsive Design: Ensure the UI is responsive and accessible across devices and screen sizes.

Educational Resources: Include tooltips or informational modals that explain complex blockchain concepts, guiding users who may be unfamiliar with dApps.

Testing and Deployment

Testing the UI: Use tools like Jest and React Testing Library to test UI components and their interactions with the blockchain.

Deploying the dApp: Once the UI is complete, deploy it using platforms like Vercel, Netlify, or traditional web hosting services. Ensure your deployed dApp can interact with the deployed smart contracts.

In this chapter, we covered the essentials of building user interfaces for decentralized applications. By leveraging popular frameworks and following best practices in design and user experience, developers can create engaging and intuitive dApps. A well-crafted UI not only enhances user satisfaction but also encourages wider adoption of blockchain technology. As dApps continue to grow, mastering UI development will be a vital skill for developers in the blockchain ecosystem.

Chapter 15: Testing Smart Contracts

Importance of Testing

Testing smart contracts is critical to ensuring their functionality, security, and reliability. Given the immutable nature of blockchain, any bugs or vulnerabilities can lead to significant financial losses and damage to user trust. This chapter outlines best practices for effectively testing smart contracts, including methodologies, tools, and strategies.

Testing Methodologies

Unit Testing: Focuses on individual components or functions of the smart contract. Each function is tested in isolation to verify its expected behavior.
Integration Testing: Tests how different components of the dApp interact with each other and with external systems, including oracles and other contracts.
End-to-End Testing: Simulates user interactions with the entire system, from the front-end UI through the smart contracts and back, ensuring the whole dApp functions as intended.
Regression Testing: Ensures that new code changes do not introduce new bugs in existing functionalities.

Tools for Testing Smart Contracts

Truffle: A popular development framework that includes built-in testing capabilities using Mocha and Chai. It allows for writing and executing tests easily.

Hardhat: A development environment that offers comprehensive testing features. It includes built-in support for Solidity debugging and can run tests using Mocha.

Remix IDE: An online IDE that supports unit testing for smart contracts. It allows for quick prototyping and testing without requiring a full development setup.

Ganache: A personal blockchain for Ethereum development. It allows developers to deploy contracts, run tests, and inspect the state of their blockchain.

Writing Tests in Truffle

Set Up a Testing Environment: Create a new test file in the `test` directory of your Truffle project.

Import Necessary Libraries:

javascript
Copy code
```
const MyContract = artifacts.require("MyContract");
```

Write Unit Tests:

javascript
Copy code
```
contract("MyContract", (accounts) => {
let myContract;

beforeEach(async () => {
myContract = await MyContract.new();
});

it("should store the value correctly", async () => {
await myContract.set(42);
const result = await myContract.get();
assert.equal(result.toString(), "42", "The value was not stored correctly.");
});
});
```

Run Tests:

bash
Copy code
```
truffle test
```

Best Practices for Testing

Use Descriptive Test Cases: Name tests clearly to indicate what functionality they validate. This aids in understanding and maintaining the test suite.

Test Edge Cases: Ensure that tests cover various scenarios, including edge cases and potential failure points.

Automate Testing: Integrate your testing framework with Continuous Integration (CI) tools like GitHub Actions or Travis CI to run tests automatically on code changes.

Gas Usage Testing: Measure the gas consumption of functions to ensure efficiency and stay within reasonable limits.

Regular Updates: Keep your test suite updated as the codebase evolves. Refactor tests alongside code changes to maintain relevance and effectiveness.

Security Testing

Static Analysis: Use tools like MythX, Slither, or Oyente to analyze code for common vulnerabilities without executing it.

Formal Verification: For critical contracts, consider using formal verification tools that mathematically prove the correctness of the code against its specifications.

Fuzz Testing: Employ fuzz testing to input random data into your contracts to identify unexpected behaviors or vulnerabilities.

In this chapter, we emphasized the importance of thorough testing in smart contract development. By adopting various testing methodologies and utilizing the right tools, developers can significantly enhance the reliability and security of their contracts. As blockchain technology continues to evolve, robust testing practices will remain a cornerstone of successful dApp development, ensuring a safe and trustworthy experience for users.

Chapter 16: Best Practices for Smart Contract Development

Importance of Best Practices

Implementing best practices in smart contract development is essential to ensure security, maintainability, and efficiency. Given the potential risks associated with blockchain technology, adhering to established guidelines can mitigate vulnerabilities and enhance the overall quality of decentralized applications (dApps). This chapter outlines key best practices for developing robust smart contracts.

Code Clarity and Documentation

Write Clear Code: Use meaningful variable and function names to make the code self-explanatory. Avoid complex logic where possible.
Comment Your Code: Document important functions and complex logic sections to improve readability for future developers.
Maintain a Style Guide: Adhere to a consistent coding style, which enhances collaboration and reduces misunderstandings.

Security Considerations

Use Established Libraries: Leverage well-audited libraries like OpenZeppelin for standard functionalities (e.g., ERC20 tokens, access control).

Avoid Reentrancy: Implement the Checks-Effects-Interactions pattern to prevent reentrancy attacks.
solidity
Copy code
```
function withdraw(uint amount) public {
require(balances[msg.sender] >= amount);
balances[msg.sender] -= amount; // Update state first
payable(msg.sender).transfer(amount); // External call
}
```

Limit Gas Consumption: Optimize functions to minimize gas usage, especially for public and external functions.

Testing and Auditing

Comprehensive Testing: Develop unit, integration, and end-to-end tests to cover all functionality. Use frameworks like Truffle or Hardhat.

Conduct Code Reviews: Regularly review code with peers to catch potential issues and improve quality.

Use Automated Tools: Employ static analysis tools (e.g., Slither, MythX) to identify vulnerabilities before deployment.

Upgradeability and Maintenance

Implement Upgrade Patterns: Use patterns like the Proxy Pattern to enable future upgrades without losing state.

Plan for Maintenance: Design contracts with upgradability in mind, allowing for adjustments as requirements evolve.

Efficient Gas Management

Batch Operations: Where possible, combine multiple operations into a single transaction to save on gas fees.

Use Events for Logging: Emit events instead of storing data on-chain when possible, as events are cheaper to store and easier to track.

solidity
Copy code
```
event ValueChanged(uint newValue);
```

```
function    setValue(uint    newValue)
public {
value = newValue;
emit ValueChanged(newValue);
}
```

Decentralization and Transparency

Promote Transparency: Clearly communicate your contract's purpose and operations. Use public events and clear function visibility.
Incorporate Community Feedback: Engage with your community for feedback and suggestions, especially for governance-related changes.

Compliance and Regulations

Stay Updated on Regulations: Be aware of legal requirements concerning cryptocurrencies and smart contracts in your jurisdiction.
KYC and AML Practices: If necessary, implement Know Your Customer (KYC) and Anti-Money Laundering (AML) practices in your dApp.

In this chapter, we explored essential best practices for smart contract development. By focusing on clarity, security, efficient gas management, and thorough testing, developers can create high-quality and reliable smart contracts. Adhering to these best practices not only minimizes risks but also enhances user trust and satisfaction in the rapidly evolving blockchain ecosystem. As the industry matures, these principles will serve as the foundation for successful and sustainable dApps.

Recap of Key Concepts Covered

In this chapter, we reflect on the essential concepts we've explored throughout the book. We've journeyed through the foundational principles of blockchain technology, including:

Decentralization: Understanding how blockchain eliminates the need for a central authority, enabling peer-to-peer transactions and increasing security.

Consensus Mechanisms: We delved into various methods, such as Proof of Work and Proof of Stake, that ensure agreement among network participants.

Smart Contracts: The automation of agreements through code was discussed, highlighting their potential to revolutionize various industries.

Cryptocurrency Fundamentals: We explored the role of digital currencies in the blockchain ecosystem, their benefits, and their challenges.

Real-World Applications: From finance to supply chain management, we examined how blockchain is being utilized across different sectors.

Resources for Further Learning and Exploration

As you continue your journey into the blockchain space, consider the following resources:

Books: Titles such as "Mastering Bitcoin" by Andreas M. Antonopoulos and "Blockchain Basics" by Daniel Drescher provide deeper insights.

Online Courses: Platforms like Coursera, edX, and Udacity offer courses on blockchain development, cryptocurrency, and decentralized applications (dApps).

Podcasts: Shows like "Unchained" and "The Bad Crypto Podcast" keep you updated on the latest trends and expert interviews in the blockchain world.

Community Forums: Engage with platforms like Reddit, Stack Exchange, and GitHub to ask questions, share knowledge, and connect with fellow enthusiasts.

Meetups and Conferences: Attend local blockchain meetups and global conferences to network and learn from industry leaders.

Encouragement to Contribute to the Blockchain Community

The blockchain community thrives on collaboration and innovation. As you gain knowledge and skills, consider ways to contribute:

Open Source Projects: Join initiatives that align with your interests. Contributing to code, documentation, or even testing can provide valuable experience.

Knowledge Sharing: Write articles, create videos, or host webinars to share your insights with others. Teaching is a great way to solidify your own understanding.

Mentorship: If you become proficient in certain areas, consider mentoring newcomers. Your guidance can help others navigate their blockchain journeys.

Advocacy: Promote blockchain's potential in your networks. Helping others understand the benefits can spur broader adoption and innovation.

In closing, blockchain technology represents a transformative force in our world. Embrace the learning, stay curious, and actively engage in the community to help shape the future of this exciting field. Your contributions can make a difference!

www.ingramcontent.com/pod-product-compliance
Lightning Source LLC
Chambersburg PA
CBHW070348230526
45471CB00006B/2465